Mark H. Hoeksema

Studies in
ACTS

REFORMED
FREE PUBLISHING
ASSOCIATION

Jenison, Michigan

Scripture cited is taken from the Authorized (King James) Version

Reformed Free Publishing Association
1894 Georgetown Center Drive
Jenison MI 49428
616-457-5970
www.rfpa.org
mail@rfpa.org

Book design and typesetting by Erika Kiel

ISBN 978-1-936054-93-0
LCCN 2015952421

Introduction

Acts 1 introduces the entire book. It takes up the thread of New Testament history where the gospel narratives drop it— at the ascension of Jesus. Chapter 1 covers the events between Christ's ascension and the outpouring of the Holy Spirit, and gives an account of Jesus' ascension into heaven. In chapter 2 the book records the beginning of the acts or works of Christ through the apostles, beginning with Pentecost. Not only do these chapters furnish a historical introduction, but they also establish the connection between the gospel narratives and the subsequent history of the preaching and spread of the gospel.

Acts sets forth a three-fold theme.

First, it is the history of the work of the Holy Spirit. Luke's first gospel narrative of the life of Jesus was definitely Christ-centered, as recounted by his history of the life of Christ. During his life Christ promised his people that the Spirit would be poured out on them. In Acts we see the fulfillment of that promise. These two, however, are not contradictory, since the Holy Spirit is the Spirit of Christ, who always speaks of Christ and who works the works of Christ.

Second, Acts sets forth the doctrine of the church, which in its simplicity is a model for the organization and operation of the church as guided by the Spirit.

Third, Acts is eminently evangelistic. That is, it records the history of the preaching and the spread of the gospel through the preaching of the word and the witnessing by believers to the salvation of Jesus Christ through the work of the Spirit.

In all of these ways, Acts serves as a paradigm for the New Testament church throughout its history, even to the present.

The Writer

The author of Acts is the Holy Spirit. Acts is divinely inspired and belongs to the canon of scripture. Luke is the writer. We do not know a great deal about Luke, perhaps because his identity and character must take a subordinate place to the content of his writing. The point is not who wrote, but what he wrote. We know that Luke was the writer of the gospel according to Luke: the account of the life, the teaching, and the deeds of Jesus.

Luke was neither one of the twelve disciples nor one of the apostles. However, he frequently accompanied the apostle Paul on parts of his missionary journeys, as is evident from the passages in Acts in which Luke uses the first person plural pronoun "we" to indicate his accompanying of Paul.

Whether he was an eyewitness of what he records, or whether he is the recorder of the history of the early church as it was told to him by others, in his writing we have an accurate history of the early church and the spread of the gospel throughout the then-known world.

We do know that Luke was an educated man, which helps lend credence to his writing. Colossians 4:14 identifies him as a doctor, an occupation that required education, as it does today. Also, his use of the Greek language exhibits the mark of a learned man. We do not know for certain if he was a Jew or a Gentile, although many scholars think he was a Jew, based on his obvious acquaintance with the Old Testament.

Methodology

This is a study guide, not a commentary. It therefore does not take a statement or an explanation format, but a question format, which is intended to help God's people understand the history recorded in Acts not from a merely formal viewpoint, but also the significance of the history as it records the work of the Holy Spirit in teaching us the doctrine of the church. I have therefore deliberately asked the often difficult "why" and "how" questions in order to foster an understanding of this scripture. As much as possible the questions are intentionally leading, interspersed with minimal remarks, with the goal of provoking study, discussion, and thought, thus to assist in the understanding of Acts, whether in Bible study societies or on a personal level. To the extent that the questions are accurately answered in the light of scripture, the student of Acts will gain an understanding of the epistle.

Suggested Study Resources

Gordon G. Keddie, *You Are My witnesses*, Evangelical Press USA.

Derek W. K. Thomas, *Acts: Reformed Expository Commentary*, P&R Publishing.

R. C. Sproul, *Acts: St. Andrew's Expositional Commentary*, Crossway.

F. F. Bruce, *Commentary on the Book of Acts*, Eerdmans.

John Calvin, *Commentary on the book of Acts*, Eerdmans.

Some of these books can be obtained used either online or from a used book store. A good Bible dictionary or encyclopedia will also be helpful.

Acts 1

Acts 1:1–5

Luke does not formally introduce Acts, but begins by immediately reminding Theophilus concerning his former treatise.

1. Who was Theophilus? What does his name mean? Do we know anything else about him?

2. What is "the former treatise"?

3. What was the content of the former treatise? What was its purpose (Luke 1:4)?

4. What is the implication of the word *began*?

5. Is the book's title *The Acts of the Apostles* accurate? Can you suggest a better one?

6. What was the function of the apostles? What was a requirement to be an apostle (v. 2)?

7. What was the purpose of the forty days (vv. 2–3)?

8. What is meant by "infallible proofs"? Is it possible that there were more appearances of Christ than the ten recorded in scripture?

9. What is the significance of the fact that the period between the resurrection and the ascension was forty days in duration?

10. Where were the disciples assembled? Why were they not to leave Jerusalem (v. 4)?

11. What was "the promise of the Father" (v. 4)? When had they heard it from Jesus (John 14–17)?

12. What is the baptism with the Holy Ghost (v. 5)? What was the difference between John's baptism and the baptism with the Holy Ghost?

13. Why does Jesus mention John's baptism?

14. Is there reason here to reject water baptism in favor of Spirit baptism?

15. Is there an essential difference between John's baptism and Jesus' baptism (Acts 19:1–6)?

Acts 1:6–8

These verses contain the conversation between Jesus and his disciples immediately prior to his ascension from the Mount of Olives.

1. What does the question of the disciples (v. 6) indicate concerning their understanding of Jesus and his kingdom?

2. In what sense did they conceive of the kingdom?

3. Would they ask the same question ten days later on Pentecost? Why or why not?

4. Jesus' reply (v. 7) is not a direct answer to their question. Why does he answer as he does?

5. Does Jesus mean that after the outpouring of the Spirit, the disciples will have power (correctly: authority) to know the times and the seasons?

6. What contrast does the word *but* indicate (v. 8)?

7. What kind of power would the disciples receive? From what source? With what result?

8. In what way were the disciples to be witnesses of Jesus (v. 8)?

9. Is the fourfold geographical order mentioned in verse 8 a prophecy, a suggestion, or a commandment?

10. What is the reason for this order?

11. Is this order normative for mission work today? Why or why not?

12. If so, what are the practical implications for us?

Acts 1:9–11

These verses record the ascension of Christ.

1. What other scriptures refer to Christ's ascension?

2. What was the nature or meaning of the ascension?

3. What was the difference between this appearance of Jesus and his previous appearances?

4. What is the significance of clouds in scripture? What does it mean that a cloud received Jesus?

5. Verse 11 refers to the return of Christ at the end of time. What is the meaning of "in like manner"?

6. Why do angels appear at this time? What is the significance of their white apparel? Why is it necessary for them to appear at such times?

7. Why do the angels ask the question of verse 11?

8. What is the significance of Jesus' ascension for himself?

9. What is the significance of Jesus' ascension for the church?

Acts 1:12–14

These verses give a list of the disciples (v. 13), the women who followed Jesus (v. 14), and where they went.

1. Where did the disciples go after Christ's ascension? Why?

2. What is a Sabbath's day journey?

3. Did those named in verses 13 and 14 and the 120 of verse 15 constitute the church?

4. What characterized this assembly (v. 14)? For what did they pray?

5. Why was there a period of ten days between the ascension and Pentecost? What is the significance of the number ten?

Acts 1:15–26

These verses record Peter's speech regarding a replacement apostle for Judas Iscariot and the election of Matthias.

1. To what Old Testament passage does Peter refer in characterizing Judas (v. 16)?

2. How does Peter describe the death of Judas (v. 18)? How must we understand this?

3. How does Peter ground his argument (v. 20)? What is the meaning of bishoprick?

4. What does Peter say is a requirement to be an apostle (v. 21)?

5. What is another requirement (v. 22)?

6. Does Peter's conclusion follow from his argument?

7. In the context of this selection, what is the significance of the prayer of the apostles (vv. 24–25)?

8. To what truth(s) do the believers appeal in their prayer?

9. Was it necessary to select a replacement for Judas?

10. What is the meaning of casting lots?

11. Was the casting of lots appropriate in this situation?

12. Was this a valid selection?

13. In light of the fact that we never again read of Matthias, does this really matter?

Acts 2

Acts 2:1–4

These verses record the outpouring of the Holy Spirit on Pentecost and its accompanying signs.

1. When did Pentecost take place? What does it mean that it "was fully come" (v. 1)?

2. What was the Old Testament feast that corresponded to Pentecost? How was this true?

3. Why were the believers "with one accord in one place" (v. 1)?

4. What is the meaning of the sound of the mighty rushing wind? What is the significance of wind?

5. What does this tell us about the Holy Spirit?

6. What is the meaning of the cloven tongues like fire? What is the meaning of fire in scripture?

7. What does this tell us about the Holy Spirit?

8. What is the meaning of the speaking in tongues by the believers? Did they speak in languages unfamiliar to them or did they speak in their native Aramaic and their hearers heard in their native languages?

9. What does the speaking in tongues tell us about the Holy Spirit?

10. Is it correct to say that Pentecost is the birthday of the church? Why or why not?

11. Why is the presence of the Spirit in the church today not accompanied by the same or similar signs?

Acts 2:5–13

These verses record the reaction to the miracle of Pentecost.

1. There were many Jews living in Jerusalem. Why are they called devout men? Why does Luke mention that they came from every nation under heaven?

2. Why was there a multitude in Jerusalem at this time? Why did God choose this time to send the Holy Spirit?

3. What was the first reaction of the multitude (vv. 6, 12)? What was the reason?

4. What was the second reaction (vv. 7, 12)? How is the fact that the disciples were Galileans the reason for this reaction?

5. What was the third reaction of some in the multitude (v. 13)? Why would they say this?

6. Why are the various languages and nationalities mentioned in verses 9–11?

Acts 2:14–36

These verses record Peter's Pentecost sermon.

1. Why is Peter the one who gives this sermon?

2. How does he refute the charge of drunkenness?

3. Why does Peter begin his sermon by using the prophecy of Joel 2:28–32 to explain the events of Pentecost?

4. What are the last days (v. 17)?

5. How must we understand "all flesh" (v. 17)? How was this prophecy fulfilled on Pentecost?

6. Why is prophesying emphasized (vv. 17–18)? What is prophecy?

7. What are visions and dreams? How are these the work of the Spirit? Why are they important?

8. Why are prophecy, dreams, and visions not evidences of the Spirit's work today?

9. Who are God's servants and handmaidens?

10. When do the events of verses 19–20 take place?

11. How are these events the work of the Spirit?

12. What is "the great and notable day of the Lord" (v. 20)?

13. What does calling on the name of the Lord mean (v. 21)?

14. Why does Peter call Christ "Jesus of Nazareth" and refer to him as a man (v. 22)?

15. What does God's approval mean?

16. What are miracles? What are wonders? What are signs?

17. Who did these miracles, wonders, and signs? What is their purpose?

18. What is God's determinate counsel? What is his foreknowledge?

19. Why is Peter so accusatory in verse 23? What does this tell us about preaching?

20. In verses 24–32 Peter speaks at length of the resurrection of Jesus. Why does he emphasize the resurrection rather than other events (the incarnation, death, or ascension) in the life of Christ?

21. What does it mean that Christ could not "be holden" by death. Why is this true?

22. Why does Peter quote Psalm 16:8–11 (vv. 25–28)?

23. How does Peter show that Psalm 16 ultimately refers not to David, but to Christ (v. 29)?

24. How did David know that he spoke of Christ (v. 30)?

25. What does it mean that God swore an oath to David (v. 30)? What was the oath?

26. What conclusion does Peter draw in verse 31?

27. What is Peter's conclusion regarding the resurrection (v. 32)?

28. What conclusion does Peter draw in verse 33?

29. Why must Christ be exalted and receive the promise of the Spirit before he pours out the Spirit (v. 33)?

30. How does David prove that Psalm 110:1 refers to Christ?

31. What conclusion does Peter draw in verse 36?

32. What does it mean that Jesus is both Lord and Christ?

Acts 2:37–40

These verses record the immediate response to Peter's sermon.

1. What does being "pricked in their heart" mean? How did this happen?

2. Why did Peter's audience ask what they must do, i.e., what action must they take (v. 37)?

3. What is repentance?

4. Why was baptism necessary?

5. Is repentance and baptism a condition to receiving the Holy Spirit? If not, why not?

6. How are verses 38 and 39 ("For") related?

7. What truth is expressed by "the promise is unto you and to your children"?

8. What is "this untoward generation"?

Acts 2:41–47

These verses record the life of the early church.

1. What was the relation between receiving the word and baptism?

2. Three thousand souls were immediately added to the church. Why is this number recorded?

3. Verse 42 records the unity of the church in its many aspects. To what does breaking of bread refer (vv. 42, 46)?

4. What does it mean that "fear came upon every soul"?

5. Why were many signs and wonders performed by the apostles?

6. Does the fact that those who believed were together and had all things in common imply a communist-style life and organization of the church (vv. 44–45)?

7. Why did the early believers have all things in common?

8. Why did the believers continue in the temple, since by the outpouring of the Spirit the temple worship had been fulfilled by Christ?

9. What do "gladness and singleness of heart" mean?

10. Who were those whom God added to the church? What is the relation between those who had favor with the people and those whom God added to the church?

Acts 3

Acts 3:1–11

These verses record the first known miracle performed in the early New Testament church by Peter and John. Many other miracles were performed by the apostles.

1. Why did Peter and John go to the temple at the hour of prayer (3 PM)?

2. Why is the lame man described as being handicapped from birth (v. 2)?

3. What was the "Beautiful" gate of the temple (vv. 2, 10)? Why was the lame man daily placed at this gate? Who knew him?

4. What was the lame's man problem (v. 7)? Of what in scripture is the figure of lameness?

5. Why did Peter tell the man to look at him and John?

6. Why did Peter take the man by his right hand and lift him up?

7. Twice Luke says that he leaped; he also stood and walked. Why is this emphasized?

8. What was Solomon's porch? Is this significant?

9. What was the result of his being healed (vv. 9–10a)?

10. What was the result on the part of the healed man (v. 11)? On the part of the people?

11. What was the purpose of this miracle? What is its connection with the work of the Spirit and with the work of Christ?

Acts 3:12–26

These verses record the sermon of Peter following and explaining the miracle.

1. To whom did Peter address his remarks?

2. Why does scripture speak of Peter's answering? What was his answer? To whom did he answer?

3. Why did Peter cite the patriarchs (v. 13)?

4. Why did Peter emphasize the denial and killing of Jesus (vv. 13–15)?

5. What is the significance of the names Peter used: Holy One, Just, Prince of life?

6. Is the reference of verse 16 to Jesus or to the lame man? Or to both?

7. What was the Jews' ignorance? Was it an excuse for their denial and killing of Christ?

8. How did Peter explain their action from God's viewpoint (v. 18)?

9. What is the meaning of repentance? What are "the times of refreshing" (v. 19)?

10. In what way will God send Jesus? When was he preached before?

11. What are "the times of restitution" (v. 21)?

12. In verses 22–23 Peter quotes Deuteronomy 18:15, 19. Who was the prophet mentioned here?

13. What does it mean that this prophet will be "like unto me" (v. 22)?

14. What do all the other prophets do?

15. What does it mean that Peter's audience is composed of children of the prophets and of the covenant?

16. What is the significance of "first" (v. 26)?

17. In what way is Jesus sent to bless?

18. Who are the "every one"? Does this imply a universal atonement?

Acts 4

Acts 4:1–4

These verses record a two-fold reaction to Peter's message.

1. Negatively, who interrupted the apostles' speaking? Who were the priests? Who was the ruler of the temple? Who were the Sadducees?

2. For what two reasons were they upset (v. 2)?

3. Why is it significant that the Sadducees are mentioned in connection with Jesus' resurrection?

4. What did they do? Why?

5. Positively, what was the reaction of many of the people (v. 4)?

6. If the number of the men was about five thousand, what does this tell us about the explosive growth of the church?

Acts 4:5–12

These verses record the trial of Peter and John.

1. Who were the rulers? The elders? The scribes?

2. What do we know about Annas and Caiaphas?

3. Who were the kindred of the high priest?

4. Does the mention of these people indicate nepotism and corruption? How so?

5. What organization is implied by the mention of these people and groups?

6. What assumption did they make in their question of verse 7? Did they know the answer?

7. By what power did Peter speak (v. 8)? What does this tell us about the Holy Spirit?

8. How did Peter define the issue on his terms (v. 9) in answering the question of the Jews?

9. Why did Peter again emphasize their guilt in crucifying Jesus (v. 10)?

10. Why did Peter mention the fact of the resurrection (v. 10)?

11. How did he prove his contention from the Old Testament (v. 11)?

12. Why did Peter explain salvation in terms of the "name" (v. 12)? What does this mean?

Acts 4:13–22

These verses record the actions of the Sanhedrin and the response of Peter and John.

1. What do "ignorant" and "unlearned" mean (v. 13)? How could the authorities know this?

2. Why did their ignorance and lack of learning matter?

3. What does it mean that they noted that Peter and John had been with Jesus?

4. What could they not do (vv. 14, 16)?

5. What dilemma did they face (v. 16)?

6. What did they decide (v. 16)? Why were they worried about the people (vv. 17, 21)?

7. Did they have the authority for their commandment (v. 18)? Why or why not?

8. How did Peter and John counter this commandment (v. 19)?

9. Under what circumstances must we listen to God rather than to men?

10. Why were Peter and John compelled to speak of what they saw and heard?

11. Why does scripture mention that the lame man was more than forty years old?

Acts 4:23–31

These verses record the prayer of the church following the release of Peter and John.

1. Where did Peter and John go? What did they do (v. 23)?

2. What was the reaction of the church (v. 24)?

3. Why did the prayer of the church begin by speaking of God as the creator (v. 24)?

4. Why did the church quote David in Psalm 2:1?

5. Since Jesus grew to be an adult, lived, was crucified, died, and rose from the dead, why is he called "thy holy child Jesus" (vv. 27, 30)?

6. Three people/groups are mentioned representatively in verse 27: Herod, Pontius Pilate and the Gentiles, and the people of Israel.

7. Whom did Herod represent?

8. Whom did Pilate and the Gentiles represent?

9. Whom did the people of Israel represent?

10. What does it mean that these three did whatever God by his hand and counsel determined (v. 28)? Of what comfort is this truth to us?

11. What is the meaning of God's hand?

12. In contrast to the threatening of the Jews, for what did the church petition? Why was this necessary?

13. Why was healing, together with signs and miracles, important for the early church?

14. Why was the church's place shaken (v. 31)? What does this tell us about the Holy Spirit?

Acts 4:32–37

These verses describe the life of the early New Testament church.

1. How was the unity of the church manifest (v. 32)?

2. Why did the church have all things in common?

3. What is the great power with which the apostles witnessed of the resurrection (v. 33)?

4. What is the "great grace" of verse 33?

5. How are verses 34–35 to be understood? Is this a model for the church today? Why or why not?

6. Who was Barnabas? How is he described?

7. What is the significance of the example of Barnabas?

Acts 5

Acts 5:1–10

These verses describe the history of Ananias and Sapphira in sharp contrast to the example of Barnabas.

1. What could have motivated Ananias and Sapphira to be apparent members of the church?

2. What did they do (vv. 1–2)? What did they do with the proceeds of their sale?

3. Was it wrong for them to give only part of the sale price of their land to the apostles?

4. What was their deception? Why did they engage in this deception?

5. Without questioning Ananias, how could Peter know what they had done?

6. Why did Peter quiz Sapphira about the details of the sale and not Ananias?

7. What was their sin (vv. 4, 9)? Who motivated them to commit it?

8. How could Peter say that they had not lied to men when apparently they had done so?

9. What had Ananias conceived in his heart (v. 4)?

10. Why was his punishment so swift and severe? Did the punishment fit the crime? How?

11. Who inflicted this punishment? What was the purpose of its severity?

12. What does it mean that they had tempted the Spirit (v. 9)?

13. How must the "great fear" of verse 11 be understood?

Acts 5:12–16

These verses record the miracles performed by the apostles.

1. What are signs in scripture?

2. What are wonders?

3. How are they related?

4. How do they describe miracles?

5. What is the purpose of miracles?

6. What were the signs and wonders done by the apostles?

7. Why is Peter singled out (v. 15)?

8. The miracles done by his shadow are perhaps more amazing than Jesus' miracles. Why?

9. What was the negative effect of these miracles? Who were "the rest" (v. 13)?

10. Why did they not dare to join the church?

11. What was the positive effect of the miracles (vv. 13b–14)?

Acts 5:17–33

These verses record further confrontation between the Jewish authorities and the apostles.

1. Why are the Sadducees specifically mentioned (vv. 17, 30)?

2. What did the authorities do? Why did they take this action?

3. Why did God counteract the action of the Jews by freeing the apostles?

4. What are "the words of this life" (v. 20)?

5. What was the purpose of calling together the council or Sanhedrin (v. 21)?

6. Upon discovering that everything was as it should have been except that the apostles were missing, what was their concern (v. 24)?

7. Upon being informed that the apostles were teaching in the temple, what should have been their response?

8. Why were the authorities afraid of being stoned by the people (v. 26)?

9. After the council reminded the apostles that they had been forbidden to teach in the name of Jesus, they accused the apostles of bringing Jesus' blood upon them. What does this tell us regarding their consciences?

10. Was the accusation valid that it was the intention of the apostles to bring the blood of Jesus on the unbelieving Jews (v. 28)?

11. What principle did Peter state more forcefully than he did in Acts 4:19? Why did he do this?

12. Did Peter in verse 30 agree with the accusation of verse 28?

13. What truth did Peter emphasize in verse 30? Why?

14. What is the implied accusation in "the God of our fathers" (v. 30) and "Israel" (v. 31)?

15. What does it mean that the Holy Spirit is a witness of the death, resurrection, and exaltation of Jesus?

16. Why were the Jews so enraged by Peter's words that they wanted to kill the apostles?

17. What does this tell us regarding the nature of sin?

Acts 5:34–40

These verses record the advice of Gamaliel.

1. Who was Gamaliel? What was his reputation?

2. Why was his advice given without the presence of the apostles (v. 34)?

3. What was his warning (v. 35)? What two examples of caution did he give?

4. Who was Theudas? What was the result of his actions? How did this example prove his point?

5. Who was Judas of Galilee? What did he do? What was the result of his rebellion?

6. What was the essence of Gamaliel's advice (v. 38)? What did he mean by refraining from the apostles?

7. How must we evaluate Gamaliel's advice? Was it a matter of principle, or was it pragmatic and utilitarian?

8. From the viewpoint of the Jews, was their "hands off" policy good advice? Why or why not?

9. If the Jews' policy was neutral, why did they beat the apostles (v. 40)?

Acts 5:41–42

These words record the attitude and action of the apostles after their confrontation with the authorities.

1. Why did the apostles rejoice? How can persecution be a matter of rejoicing?

2. In obedience to the Spirit, what did they do?

3. How are both their attitude and their action models for the church today?

Acts 6

Acts 6:1–8

These verses record the institution of the office of deacon and the increase of the church.

1. What are the "those days" of verse 1? When was the number of the disciples multiplied?

2. What problem arose?

3. Who were the Grecians?

4. Who were the Hebrews?

5. What were the "daily ministrations"?

6. Why did this problem concern the widows in the church?

7. How and why could this happen (v. 2b)?

8. How did the twelve apostles solve this problem?

9. Seven men were chosen by the church (v. 5). How were they nominated (v. 3)?

10. What does this tell us regarding the deacons and their election?

11. What is the meaning of the laying on of hands?

12. What is this model for the church today? How so?

13. What was the result of this expansion of the church as it began to take a more organizational character (v. 7)?

14. What are the requirements of the office of deacon (v. 3)?

15. How was Stephen able to do great wonders and miracles among the people?

Acts 6:9–15

These verses record the Jews' false witness against Stephen.

1. Various groups are mentioned as being opposed to Stephen's teachings.

2. What was the synagogue of the Libertines?

3. Who were the Cyrenians? Who were the Alexandrians? Who were the Cilicians and Asians?

4. What were they unable to do? Why not?

5. What did they do instead (vv. 11, 13)?

6. What were the blasphemous words of which they accused Stephen?

7. How did the Jews misinterpret the words of Jesus? (v. 14)?

8. If true, why was this such a serious accusation?

9. Upon hearing these accusations, Stephen's face became like that of an angel. How is this to be understood?

10. Why did this happen?

Acts 7

Acts 7:1–53

These verses contain the sermon of Stephen.

1. How did the high priest give Stephen an opportunity to defend himself against the accusations made against him (v. 1)?

2. Why did he not immediately defend himself directly against his accusers?

3. Why did Stephen defend himself by reviewing the history of the church from Abraham to Christ?

4. In the history of Abraham (vv. 2–8), what did Stephen emphasize? How is this his defense?

5. What is the covenant of circumcision (v. 8)?

6. Why did Stephen use the example of Joseph (vv. 9–19)?

7. What was Stephen's emphasis in recounting this history?

8. What was Stephen's purpose in his lengthy recounting of the history of Moses (vv. 20–41)?

9. To whom did Stephen refer in verse 37?

10. Who was in the church in the wilderness (v. 38)?

11. Who was the angel who spoke at Sinai? What were the lively oracles (v. 38)?

12. What is Stephen's point in recounting the rebellion and idolatry of Israel (vv. 39–41)?

13. What is the reference of verses 42–43?

14. Who was Moloch? Who was Remphan?

15. What was Israel's punishment for their idolatry?

16. Stephen spoke next of the tabernacle and the temple (vv. 44–51). What was the tabernacle of witness (v. 44)?

17. Why did Stephen say that the fathers brought the tabernacle into Canaan with Jesus (correct: Joshua)?

18. Stephen spoke of the temple of David and Solomon (vv. 45–47), and immediately added that God does not dwell in temples made with hands (vv. 48–50). Is this a contradiction? Why or why not?

Acts 7:54–60

These verses record the details of the death of Stephen.

1. How did Stephen's accusation follow from the rest of his speech?

2. What does "stiffnecked" mean?

3. What is the meaning of being uncircumcised in heart and ears?

4. What does it mean to resist the Holy Spirit? How did the Jews and their fathers do this (v. 51)?

5. How did Stephen connect the fathers' killing of the prophets and the Jews' killing of Christ (v. 52)?

6. Why did he call Jesus "the Just One"?

7. Of what did Stephen accuse his accusers (v. 52)?

8. Why was his accusation of verse 53 significant?

9. What does "the disposition of angels" mean?

10. Why were the authorities so angry (v. 54)?

11. What is the connection between Stephen's being full of the Spirit and his seeing the glory of God and seeing Jesus standing on the right hand of God?

12. Why is Jesus described as standing rather than sitting on God's right hand?

13. What does the lack of a formal verdict on the part of the Jews indicate?

14. Why did the Jews stop their ears (v. 57)?

15. How could the Jews stone Stephen without the permission of the Roman authorities?

16. Of what were the words of Stephen in verse 59 reminiscent?

17. Why did Stephen speak with a loud voice?

18. Why did Stephen ask God not to lay this sin to his murderers' charge (v. 60)?

19. Stephen met with a violent end. Why then do we read that he "fell asleep"?

20. What is the significance of the mention of Saul's (Paul's) participation in Stephen's death?

Acts 8

Acts 8:1–4

These verses describe the initial persecution of the early church.

1. How does verse 2 conclude the history of Stephen?

2. Verses 1 and 3 pick up the thread (7:58) of the activity of Saul. What does it mean that he consented to Stephen's death?

3. Who were the authors of the persecution of the church at Jerusalem (v. 1)?

4. How did Saul persecute the church (v. 3)?

5. What does this tell us about his position?

6. How could he engage in such persecution without the apparent consent of the Roman authorities?

7. Where did the Christians go as the result of this persecution?

8. How did this fulfill the command of Jesus in Acts 1:8?

9. What was the result of this persecution (v. 4)?

10. Why did the apostles remain at Jerusalem?

11. What was the unanticipated (on the part of the Jews) result (v. 1, cf. Acts 1:8)?

Acts 8:5–8

These verses record the preaching and miracles of Philip.

1. Where was Samaria located?

2. What do we know about the religion of the Samaritans?

3. What do we know about Philip?

4. What did Philip preach (vv. 5, 12)?

5. Why did Philip perform the miracles mentioned in verses 6–7? Could this have been connected with the deeds of Simon?

6. What was the reaction of the people to Philip's preaching and the accompanying miracles?

Acts 8:6–25

These verses record the history of Simon the sorcerer and his interaction with the apostles.

1. Who was Simon and what did he do?

2. Specifically, what is sorcery?

3. What does it mean that he bewitched the people?

4. What does it mean that he gave himself out as some great one?

5. How did the people of Samaria view him (v. 10)?

6. Was Simon able to do actual miracles, or did he cleverly deceive the people?

7. Why did the people respect him (v. 11)?

8. What is meant by "the things concerning the kingdom and the name of Jesus Christ"?

9. How is this contrasted with Simon's activities?

10. Did Simon really believe or did he fake his faith?

11. Did Simon fool Philip by being baptized?

12. Why did Simon shadow Philip (v. 13)?

13. Why did the apostles in Jerusalem send Peter and John to Samaria (v. 15)?

14. Why had the believers in Samaria not yet received the Spirit (v. 16)?

15. What is the connection between the laying on of hands and the outpouring of the Spirit (v. 17)?

16. Was the presence of Peter and John necessary for the outpouring of the Spirit?

17. What is the name of the sin described in verses 18–19?

18. Why did Simon want the ability to give the Spirit?

19. How did Peter rebuke him (vv. 20–23)?

20. Was Peter doubtful as to Simon's forgiveness?

21. What is meant by the gall of bitterness (v. 23)?

22. What is meant by the bond of iniquity?

23. Does Simon's request in verse 24 indicate that he was a true believer, or was he merely trying to avoid the consequences of his sin?

24. Why do we not read further of the outcome of this matter?

25. In contrast to Simon's actions, what did the apostles do (v. 25)?

Acts 8:26–40

These verses record the history of Philip and the Ethiopian eunuch.

1. Where was Philip instructed to go and for what purpose?

2. Why is it mentioned that this area was desert?

3. What can be said about the history and religion of the country of Ethiopia?

4. What do we know about the Ethiopian man?

5. How can it be explained that he had been to Jerusalem to worship (v. 27)?

6. How can it be explained that a man of such stature was apparently returning to his country alone?

7. How did the Spirit speak to Philip?

8. What made Philip ask the eunuch if he understood what he was reading?

9. What scripture was the Ethiopian reading? What language was he reading?

10. Was he reading aloud (v. 30)? Why?

11. Did the eunuch suspect that Philip might be able to explain Isaiah to him (v. 31)?

12. What was the eunuch's problem (v. 34)?

13. What was the content of Philip's preaching (v. 35)?

14. For what did the eunuch ask at an oasis (v. 36)?

15. What is the requirement for adult baptism (v. 37)?

16. Is there any requirement other than believing that Jesus is the Son of God?

17. Verse 38 apparently describes baptism by immersion. Is this method a requirement? Why or why not?

18. Why did the Spirit cause Philip to vanish (v. 39)?

19. What did the eunuch do? Is there any evidence of a later church in Ethiopia, perhaps as a result of this encounter?

20. What did Philip do? Why is he called an evangelist (Acts 21:8)?

Acts 9

Acts 9:1–9

These verses record the conversion of Saul.

1. What does the mention of Damascus (v. 2) tell us about the spread of the early church?

2. Why did the church spread so rapidly (v. 1)?

3. What was Saul's intention (v. 1)? On what authority was he acting?

4. What was the light that shone around him (v. 3)?

5. Who spoke to him and what did he say?

6. In view of his later apostleship, why is this appearance important?

7. How did Saul know that it was the Lord speaking to him (v. 5)?

8. What does it mean to kick against the pricks? Why is this hard?

9. What does Saul's question in verse 6 indicate?

10. Why did the men with him hear the voice but not see the light (v. 7)?

11. Why was Saul struck blind?

12. After being led to Damascus, why did he not eat or drink for three days?

13. Is Saul's conversion normative in the church? Why or why not?

14. Why was his conversion so spectacular?

Acts 9:10–22

These verses record the events following Saul's conversion.

1. Who was Ananias?

2. What is a vision? How was a conversation possible in a vision?

3. What were the Lord's instructions to Ananias?

4. For what did Saul pray (v. 11)?

5. What did the Lord do to prepare Saul to receive Ananias (v. 12)?

6. What was Ananias' objection to the Lord's instruction? Was this valid and understandable (vv. 13–14)?

7. Why did the Lord immediately mention Saul's suffering for his name's sake (v. 16)? How did this come true?

8. When Ananias went to see Saul, why did he put his hands on Saul?

9. Why did Ananias address him as "Brother" (v. 17)? What does this tell us about his attitude?

10. How could Ananias know that it was Jesus who appeared to Saul on the Damascus road?

11. How did Saul receive the Holy Spirit (v. 17)?

12. After Saul received his sight (v. 18), why was he baptized? Why was this necessary?

13. Why did Saul preach that Christ was the Son of God in the synagogues in Damascus?

14. What was the reaction of the Jews at Damascus (v. 21)?

15. What does it mean that Saul increased in strength (v. 22)?

16. What does it mean that Saul confounded the Jews at Damascus? How did he prove that Jesus was the Christ?

Acts 9:23–31

These verses record the further results of Saul's conversion.

1. What is the reference to the "many days" of verse 23? Could this refer to the three years that Saul spent in Arabia (Gal. 1:17–18)?

2. What was the reaction of the Jews in Damascus? What did they do?

3. How did the disciples foil the plan of the Jews?

4. What was the reaction of the disciples at Jerusalem to Saul's efforts?

5. How did Barnabas solve this problem (v. 27)?

6. What was the content of Saul's bold speaking?

7. Who were the Grecians? Why were they angry enough to want to kill Saul (v. 29)?

8. When the disciples learned of their intention, what did they do? Why?

9. What was another reason for Saul's going to Tarsus (Acts 22:17–22)?

10. What was the connection between Saul's departure and the period of rest for the churches (v. 31)?

11. Why was it necessary and important for the churches to have this rest?

Acts 9:32–35

These verses record the healing of Aneas and lay the groundwork for the spread of the gospel to the Gentiles.

1. What does it mean that Peter passed through all quarters? What was his purpose in doing this?

2. Where was Lydda (Lod)?

3. What was the palsy that afflicted Aneas? Why is it mentioned that he had had the palsy for eight years?

4. What was the symbolic significance of his illness?

5. With what words did Peter show who is the author of the miracle?

6. Why did Peter tell Aneas to make his bed?

7. Did the people turn to the Lord because of this miracle? Why or why not?

Acts 9:36–43

These verses record the raising of Dorcas.

1. What is the meaning of her name?

2. What does it mean that she was full of good works?

3. What is the meaning of almsdeeds? What were the almsdeeds that Dorcas did (v. 39)?

4. Who were the objects of her charity (vv. 39, 41)?

5. After her death, why was her body washed and put in a room rather than being buried?

6. Knowing that Peter was in Lydda, only ten miles away from Joppa (Jaffa), what did they do?

7. For what purpose did they send for Peter? What did they expect him to do?

8. Why did Peter remove everyone from the room where Dorcas was (v. 40)?

9. For what did Peter pray?

10. How is it to be explained that Tabitha obeyed Peter's command (v. 40)?

11. Why are the widows of the church mentioned specifically (v. 41)?

12. What was the result of this miracle?

13. The occupation of Simon the tanner was unclean, according to Old Testament law. Why then did Peter live with him for many days?

14. By the healing of Aneas and the raising of Dorcas, for what was God preparing the disciples, and especially Peter, a leader among the disciples?

Acts 10

Acts 10:1–48

This chapter records Peter's interaction with Cornelius, the beginning of the inclusion of the Gentiles in the early church.

1. What are we told about Cornelius? What position did he occupy? Where was he posted? Where was Caesareus?

2. What are we told about Cornelius and his household (v. 2)?

3. How is it to be explained that he was a devout man, gave much alms, and prayed to God?

4. Was he a proselyte? For what did he pray?

5. What is the vision that Cornelius saw evidently (clearly) at 3PM? Who was the angel of the Lord?

6. Upon the angel's getting his attention by calling him by name, why was Cornelius afraid?

7. How did Cornelius know that it was the Lord who spoke to him (v. 4)?

8. What does it mean that Cornelius' prayers and alms came up as a memorial before God?

9. What did the angel command Cornelius to do (v. 5)? Why did the Lord give such precise directions (vv. 5–6)?

10. How did Cornelius obey the Lord's command (vv. 7–8)?

11. As the emissaries from Cornelius approached Caesarea, what did Peter do (v. 9)? Why did Peter pray at noon?

12. Why does scripture note that Peter was very hungry (v. 10)?

13. What is the meaning of a trance? Is it different from a vision? In what way?

14. What did Peter see? What did these creatures have in common?

15. What was the difference between clean and unclean creatures in the Old Testament?

16. What was Peter commanded to do? How was this connected with his hunger?

17. What was Peter's response (v. 14)? How is this to be evaluated?

18. What further command did the voice of the Lord give Peter (v. 15)?

19. Why was this done three times before the sheet disappeared into heaven?

20. When did the messengers from Cornelius arrive (v. 17)? What was the significance of this timing?

21. How did the Spirit speak to Peter? Why did the Spirit instruct Peter to go with the men from Cornelius instead of letting events show Peter the meaning of the vision?

22. What did the Spirit allow Peter to figure out for himself (v. 21)?

23. What reason did the messengers give for asking Peter to go to Caesarea? What are the words that Cornelius wanted to hear?

24. Who were waiting for Peter (vv. 24, 27)? What is the significance of this?

25. Why did Cornelius bow to Peter and worship him?

26. What was Peter's reaction (v. 26)? What was his reason?

27. Of what did Peter remind Cornelius (v. 28)?

28. How did Peter show that he understood the meaning of his vision (v. 28)?

29. What question did Peter repeat (v. 29)?

30. What was the answer of Cornelius? (vv. 30–33)? What did he expect (v. 33)?

31. What does it mean that God is not a respecter of persons (v. 34)?

32. How did Peter show that he understood that the gospel must be universally preached (v. 35)?

33. Why did Peter emphasize that the apostles were witnesses of the resurrection (vv. 39, 41)?

34. What was the word that God sent? What does it mean that God preached peace through Jesus Christ (v. 36)?

35. After tracing the history of Jesus, what conclusion did Peter draw (v. 43)? How did he connect the gospel of Christ with the Old Testament?

36. How was the remission of sins to be received (v. 43)?

37. What does it mean that the Spirit fell on those assembled (v. 44)? What was the evidence of this outpouring (v. 46)?

38. What is the connection between the Spirit and the word (v. 44)?

39. Why were the Jews in this group so astonished? Why is this understandable?

40. What is the relation between baptism and the Spirit (v. 47)?

41. Why did Peter stay in Caesarea for a number of days?

Acts 11

Acts 11:1–18

These verses record Peter's report to the church at Jerusalem.

1. What prompted this report (v. 1)?

2. Of what did the other apostles and the disciples accuse Peter?

3. How are they described (v. 2)?

4. Was this accusation correct? Was it justified?

5. What does this tell us about the early New Testament church?

6. Why did Peter recount logically and in detail the events concerning himself and Cornelius (vv. 4–15)?

7. What argument did Peter use to demonstrate that also the Gentiles are saved (v. 15)?

8. What second and closely connected argument does he use in verse 16?

9. What was Peter's third argument (v. 17)?

10. What was the reaction of the church at Jerusalem? Why did they hold their peace (v. 18)?

11. In light of the evidence given by Peter, what conclusion did the church draw?

Acts 11:19–30

These verses record the shifting of the center of the church from Jerusalem to Antioch. The geography begins to be increasingly important here.

1. How does Luke recap the history surrounding the death of Stephen?

2. Where was Phoenicia (today: Syria)?

3. Where was Cyprus?

4. Where was Cyrene (today: Libya)?

5. To whom was the gospel preached by those who were scattered (v. 19)? Why?

6. What is the significance of all of these countries with regard to the preaching of the gospel?

7. Who were the Grecians (v. 20)?

8. When the church in Jerusalem heard about the conversion of many in various places, what did they do (v. 22)?

9. Why did the church at Jerusalem send Barnabas to Antioch, but no farther (v. 22)?

10. What is meant by the grace of God (v. 23)?

11. In what glowing terms is Barnabas described (v. 24)? Why?

12. Why did Barnabas bring Saul from Tarsus to Antioch?

13. To what purpose did Barnabas and Saul spend a whole year in Antioch? What was the result of their labors (v. 26)?

14. Where and by whom were the disciples first called Christians (v. 26)? Was this an insult or a compliment? Does the fact that this occurred in Antioch tell us anything about this name?

15. Was the office of prophet still in existence in the New Testament church (v. 27)?

16. What was the office of prophet?

17. What did Agabus prophesy? How and when was this fulfilled?

18. What was the reaction of the disciples (v. 29–30)? What does this tell us about the unity of the early church? What does this tell us about the church today?

Acts 12

Acts 12:1–25

These verses record the history of Herod's persecution of the church, Peter's deliverance, and Herod's subsequent death.

1. About what time did the persecution described (vv. 1–2) take place?

2. Herod was not a name, but a title. Which Herod is mentioned in verse 1?

3. What was his ancestry? Over what area did he reign?

4. What was his attitude toward and his relationship with the Jews?

5. Why did Herod persecute the apostles? Whom did he kill? Why?

6. Why did Herod imprison Peter? Why did he do so at the time of the Passover (v. 3)?

7. What is a quaternion (v. 4)? How else was Peter restrained (v. 7)? Why did Herod guard Peter so heavily?

8. What was Herod's intention? Why?

9. For what did the church pray constantly? What was the relation between their praying and Peter's deliverance?

10. In light of the fact that Peter was sleeping soundly, was he worried? Why not?

11. Who was the angel who delivered Peter (v. 7)?

12. What was the sequence of events in Peter's release (vv. 7–10)?

13. What did Peter think was taking place?

14. When did Peter figure out what had happened to him? What does it mean that he came to himself (v. 11)?

15. What was the expectation of the Jews (v. 11)?

16. Where did Peter go? Why?

17. If we put ourselves in Peter's shoes, was there biblical humor in the interaction between Peter and Rhoda (vv. 13–16)?

18. After describing his deliverance from prison, what did Peter command? Who is the James of verse 17?

19. Where did Peter go? Why?

20. What was the reaction of the soldiers (v. 18)? Is this a classic understatement?

21. What was Herod's action upon Peter's disappearance? What does this tell us about Herod?

22. Why did Herod go from Judea to Caesarea in Tyre and Sidon? Why was he highly displeased?

23. How was this issue resolved (v. 20)?

24. What did Herod subsequently do (v. 21)?

25. What is the meaning of "a set day" (v. 21)?

26. What was the royal apparel in which Herod arrayed himself?

27. What was likely the content of his oration?

28. What was Herod attempting to do by means of his royal apparel and his oration?

29. What was the reaction of the people (v. 22)? How could they be so deceived?

30. If the people called Herod a god and not a man, why did God strike Herod down (v. 23)?

31. Why is it emphasized that the angel of the Lord smote Herod immediately?

32. Who smote Herod?

33. What was Herod's punishment? How was it appropriate?

34. What was the result of these events for the church (v. 24)?

35. Why did Barnabas and Saul return from Jerusalem to Antioch (v. 25)?

36. Who was John Mark?

Acts 13

Acts 13:1–3

These verses record the commission of Paul and Barnabas to preach the gospel to the Gentiles.

1. What do the people mentioned in verse 1 tell us about the universal character of the church at Antioch?

2. What is the significance of Simon's Latin nickname Niger? What does this tell us about his possible country of origin? Could he have been the Simon who carried Jesus' cross?

3. What can be known about Lucius?

4. Who was Manaen? What does it mean that he was brought up with Herod the tetrarch (Herod Antipas)?

5. What truth of scripture is illustrated by this relationship?

6. What is the difference between prophets and teachers (v. 1)?

7. What does it mean that they ministered to the Lord (v. 2)?

8. What is meant by fasting? Why did the church do this?

9. What is the connection between fasting and the command of the Spirit?

10. How did this command come to the church (v. 1)?

11. What was the laying on of hands in connection with the sending away of Barnabas and Paul?

Acts 13:4–14:28

These verses record the history of Paul's first missionary journey (AD 47–48).

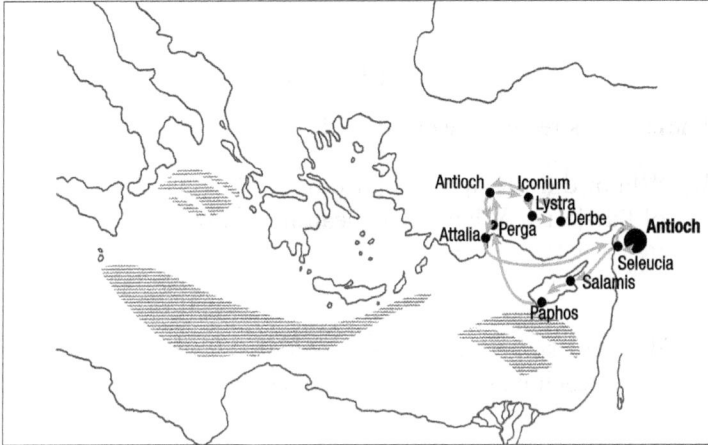

Acts 13:4–5

These verses record the apostles' first stop at Salamis.

1. Why did they go first to Cyprus?

2. What does it mean that they had "John Mark to their minister"?

3. Why did the apostles go first to the synagogue of the Jews to preach the word? Why did this become their regular practice?

4. Was there any fruit on their labors in the establishment of a church?

Acts 13:6–12

These verses record the events at Paphos.

1. Whom did the apostles encounter? What is the meaning of Bar-jesus? What is the meaning of Elymas?

2. What is a sorcerer? Why is it noted that he was a Jew? What is the teaching of the Old Testament regarding sorcery?

3. Who was Sergius Paulus? What office did he hold?

4. Why did Elymas associate with Sergius Paulus?

5. What does it mean that Sergius Paulus was a prudent man? How did he show this (v. 7)?

6. Why did Paul use such severe language toward Elymas (v. 10)?

7. What was the connection between Paul's being filled with the Spirit (v. 9) and his words?

8. What judgment did Paul call down on Elymas (v. 11)?

9. What is the significance of this blindness? Why was this blindness temporary?

10. What was the reaction of Sergius Paulus? Why was he astonished at the doctrine of the Lord rather than at the miraculous punishment of Elymas?

11. Is there any evidence that a church was established at Paphos?

12. Is there reason that beginning here, Luke uses the apostle's Roman name instead of his Jewish name?

Acts 13:13–52

These verses record the apostles' trip through Perga to Antioch in Pisidia.

1. What is the only noteworthy event in Perga? Why did John Mark return to Jerusalem?

2. Why did the apostles go to the synagogue? Why did they sit down?

3. What does verse 15 tell us about the Jews' worship?

4. What prompted the Jews to invite the apostles to speak?

5. Why did Paul address them as he did? Was there a difference between the men of Israel and those who feared God (v. 16)?

6. Why did Paul summarize the history of Israel in verses 17–22? Did not the Jews already know all of this?

7. Why did Paul stop his summary with David (v. 22)?

8. How did Paul describe Jesus (v. 23)?

9. Why did Paul include John the Baptist and his preaching (v. 24)?

10. What was Paul's point in verse 25?

11. What contrast did Paul draw between his audience and the people and rulers at Jerusalem (vv. 26–27)?

12. What does it mean that the Jews did not know Jesus? What does it mean that they did not know the prophets (v. 27)?

13. How did Paul describe the fulfillment of prophecy regarding Jesus (vv. 27–29)?

14. What was Paul's central point in his sermon (vv. 30–39)?

15. Why does he emphasize the fact that Jesus' resurrection was confirmed by witnesses (v. 31)?

16. What was Paul's line of reasoning concerning the fulfillment of prophecy regarding David and Christ (vv. 33–37)? How did he apply David's prophecies to Christ?

17. How did Paul describe the forgiveness of sins and justification (vv. 38–39)?

18. With what sharp admonition did Paul conclude his sermon? Whom did he quote?

19. After the Jews left the synagogue, what was the reaction of the Gentiles (v. 42)? For what did they ask? When?

20. What was the reaction of many Jews and proselytes (v. 43)?

21. How is it to be explained that almost the whole city came together on the next Sabbath to hear the apostles (v. 44)?

22. Why were the Jews envious (v. 45)? How did their envy come to expression in blasphemy? What is the meaning of blasphemy?

23. When did the apostles turn from the Jews to the Gentiles? What is Paul's justification for so doing (vv. 46–47)?

24. What was the reaction of the Gentiles to the gospel (v. 48)? What truth is described in this verse?

25. What was the reaction of the Jews (v. 50)? Why did they target the influential people of the city?

26. After being the objects of persecution and opposition, where did the apostles go next (vv. 50–51)?

27. What is the symbolism of shaking off the dust of the feet when they left (v. 51)?

Acts 14

Acts 14:1–6

These verses record the events at Iconium.

1. Where did the apostles go and what did they do (v. 1)?

2. What was the result?

3. How could the Greeks (Gentiles) believe if the apostles spoke in the synagogue?

4. What was the reaction of the unbelieving Jews (v. 2)? What does it mean that their minds were evil affected against the brethren?

5. Why did the apostles stay and preach so long in Iconium (v. 3)?

6. Why did the Lord enable them to do signs and wonders (v. 3)?

7. What was the final result (v. 4)?

8. What was the result of the opposition to the apostles (vv. 5–6)?

9. Did Paul "chicken out" and flee, or was his departure wise on his part?

Acts 14:7–20

These verses record the events at Lystra and Derbe.

1. What did Paul do first when the apostles came to Lystra (v. 7)?

2. What did he do in support of the gospel (vv. 8–10)?

3. How could Paul perceive that the cripple had the faith to be healed (v. 9)? Was faith a condition to this healing? What is the relation between faith and healing?

4. What was the reaction of the people of Lystra to this miracle (v. 11)? What does this tell us about their religion?

5. Why did they call Barnabas "Jupiter"? Who was Jupiter?

6. Why did they call Paul "Mercury"? Who was Mercury?

7. What did the priest of Jupiter attempt to do (v. 13)?

8. How did Paul respond (v. 15)? What is the significance of the rending of clothes? How did he show that God is the true sovereign of heaven and earth (vv. 15–17)?

9. How were the Jews from Antioch and Iconium able to sway the opinion of the people of Lystra so quickly (v. 19)?

10. What was the significance/method of stoning to death in contrast to other methods?

11. Was Paul killed by stoning or was he only injured (v. 19)?

12. How must his miraculous recovery be explained (v. 20)?

Acts 14:21–28

These verses record the return of the apostles to Antioch.

1. Was there any result of the preaching of the gospel in Derbe (v. 21)?

2. Why did the apostles retrace their steps as they returned to Antioch via the cities they had visited (vv. 21–26)?

3. What is meant by their "confirming the souls of the disciples" (v. 22)?

4. What does verse 23 tell us about the church?

5. What did they do when they returned to Antioch (v. 27)? Why was this necessary? What does this tell us about the mission work of the church?

6. Why did they stay in Antioch for a long time?

Acts 15–16

Acts 15:1–35

These verses record the council of Jerusalem.

Acts 15:1–5

These verses record the dispute that led to the council of Jerusalem.

1. Who caused this dispute to arise in the church at Antioch?

2. How are they further defined (v. 5)?

3. What did they teach the Gentile brethren (v. 1)? How necessary was circumcision, according to their teaching (v. 1)?

4. What else did they teach was necessary besides circumcision (v. 5)? What did this include?

5. How is it to be explained that they taught the necessity of keeping the whole law of Moses?

6. How could they be Pharisees and teach legalism and yet be believers (v. 5)?

7. What was the reaction of Paul and Barnabas (v. 2)?

8. Why was this issue so important to them and to the whole church?

9. Why did the church send Paul and Barnabas, along with others to Jerusalem (v. 3)?

10. What did Paul and Barnabas do on their way to Jerusalem (v. 3)? Why?

11. What did they do when they arrived (v. 4)?

Acts 15:6–12

These verses record the speeches of Peter, Paul, and Barnabas.

1. Who were the members of the council (vv. 6, 12)?

2. Did the apostles and elders decide the issue, or did the entire church decide (vv. 12, 22)?

3. Was this the first synod? Why or why not?

4. What characterized the council (v. 7)? Was this necessary and proper?

5. Why did Peter emphasize that the Gentiles believed (v. 7)?

6. What choice did God make (v. 7)? What was Peter's personal testimony?

7. What was Peter's proof that the Gentiles are saved (v. 8)? Why did he refer to God as the one who knows the hearts (v. 8) and who purifies the heart (v. 9)?

8. What did Peter mean by tempting God (v. 10)?

9. What is the unbearable yoke to which he referred (v. 10)? Why did he call it unbearable?

10. In contrast with verses 1 and 5, how does God save his people (v. 11)?

11. Who are the "we" and the "they"? What was Peter's point in using this inclusive language?

12. Why did Paul and Barnabas refer to the miracles and wonders done among the Gentiles (v. 12)?

13. How did this support and prove Peter's point?

Acts 15:13–21

These verses record the speech and advice of James.

1. Who was the James who spoke when Paul and Barnabas were finished (v. 13)?

2. How did he summarize Peter's speech (v. 14)?

3. What Old Testament scripture did James use to prove his point (vv. 15–17)?

4. Why did James prove his point by quoting from the Old Testament prophets?

5. What is the significance of James' words in verse 18?

6. What was James' negative advice (v. 19)? What did he mean by not troubling the Gentiles?

7. What was his fourfold positive advice (v. 20)? What is the meaning of each of these suggested prohibitions?

8. Which of these is based on the moral law? Why did James suggest the three that were based on the ceremonial law?

9. Why did James suggest that the Gentile observe these regulations (v. 21)?

Acts 15:22–29

These verses record the decision of the council.

1. What role did the church play in the decision of the council (v. 22)?

2. Why did the council send delegates with Paul and Barnabas to Antioch (v. 22)?

3. Why did the council put its decision in writing (v. 23)?

4. What was the council's judgment regarding those who had taught the necessity of keeping the law and of circumcision (v. 24)? What does this teach us concerning good order in the church?

5. How did they know that it seemed good to the Holy Spirit (v. 28) to take the decision of verse 29?

Acts 15:30–35

These verses record the notification of the church at Antioch of the council's decisions.

1. What was the reaction of the church to the letter from the council (vv. 30–31)?

2. In what sense were Judas and Silas prophets (v. 32)? Why was this significant for the church?

3. Why did Silas remain in Antioch (v. 34)?

4. What hint does verse 35 give us regarding the size of the church at Antioch?

Acts 15:36–41

These verses record preparations for a trip, and the division between Paul and Barnabas.

1. After some days in Antioch, what suggestion did Paul make (v. 36)?

2. What was to be the purpose of this trip?

3. What was Barnabas' intention (v. 37)? Do we know his reason?

4. Why did Paul oppose Barnabas (v. 38)? Was Paul's position justified?

5. Was the sharp contention sinful on the part of either Paul or Barnabas, or on the part of both?

6. What was God's providential purpose in the separation of Paul and Barnabas?

7. Were Paul and Barnabas permanently estranged?

8. Were Paul and John Mark permanently estranged?

9. Why was Silas (Latin name: Sylvanus) an appropriate partner for Paul?

10. What does it mean that the church recommended Paul and Silas to the grace of God (v. 40)?

11. Where did Paul begin his journey and for what purpose (v. 41)? Where did he go?

12. What does it mean that he confirmed the churches (v. 41)?

Acts 16:1–18:22

These verses record Paul's second missionary journey (AD 49–52).

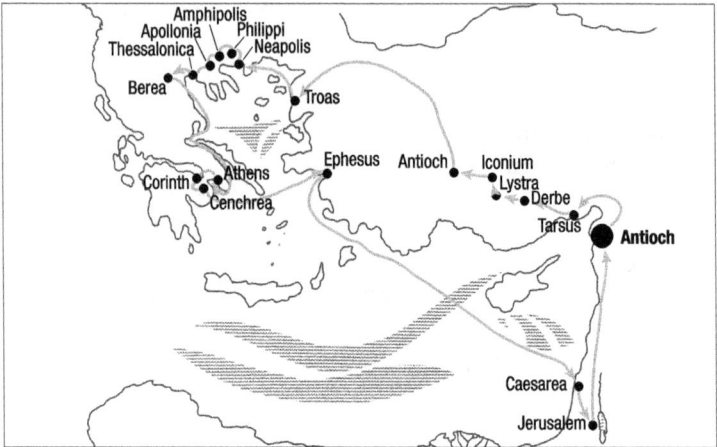

Acts 16:1–8

These verses describe the beginning of Paul's journey.

1. When he travelled to Lystra, whom did Paul meet (v. 1)?

2. Who were his mother and his grandmother? Why is it noted that his father was a Greek?

3. Why did Paul want to take him along on his journey (vv. 2–3)?

4. Why did Paul circumcise Timothy (v. 3)? How is the fact that he was known as a Gentile a reason for this action?

5. Through what cities did Paul and Silas travel (v. 4)?

6. What decrees did they deliver?

7. What was the result for the church (v. 5)?

8. What was the apparent intent of Paul and Silas (v. 6)?

9. How did the Spirit forbid them? Why?

Acts 16:9–12

These verses record the vision of the Macedonian man.

1. What is a vision (v. 9)?

2. What was the content of Paul's vision?

3. How did he know that the man was a Macedonian (v. 9)?

4. What was the request of this man (v. 9)? For what was he asking?

5. How could Paul know who he was and what he wanted?

6. Based on the use of the pronoun "we," who now had joined Paul and Silas at Troas (v. 10)?

7. What did the missionaries immediately do? How is this normative for the church today?

Acts 16:13–15

These verses record the conversion of Lydia in Philippi.

1. What do we know about the city of Philippi?

2. After being in the city for some days (v. 12), where did the missionaries go? Why was prayer made at the river in Philippi on the Sabbath (v. 13)?

3. What does Lydia's occupation as a seller of purple in Thyatira tell us about her?

4. What does it mean that the Lord opened Lydia's heart (v. 14)? What does it mean that she attended to what Paul spoke?

5. Why was the baptism of her household significant (v. 15)? What does this show?

6. On what basis did Lydia invite the missionaries into her house (v. 15)?

7. What does it mean that she constrained them (v. 15)? Why was that important for the spread of the gospel?

Acts 16:16–24

These verses record the persecution of the apostles at Philippi.

1. What was the situation of the girl who met the apostles (v. 16)?

2. What was the spirit of divination (correctly: a spirit of Python) that possessed her?

3. What is soothsaying? Since she earned her masters much money, was she accurate?

4. How is it to be explained that the evil spirit that possessed her would give the testimony of verse 17?

5. Why did the girl pester the apostles (vv. 17–18)?

6. What does it mean that Paul was grieved (v. 18)?

7. Why was Paul's command to the evil spirit successful (v. 18)?

8. What did the girl's masters do (vv. 19–20)? Why?

9. What charge was brought against Paul and Silas (vv. 20–21)?

10. Was the charge valid according to Roman law? Was it even true?

11. How did their being Jews have anything to do with this incident (v. 20)?

12. Was this persecution for the sake of the gospel or anti-Semitism?

13. Why did the magistrates tear off Paul and Silas' clothing (v. 22)?

14. Why did the magistrates skip a trial and go directly to punishment (vv. 22–23)?

15. What was the reason for the high security imprisonment described in verse 24?

Acts 16:25–34

These verses record the conversion of the Philippian jailer.

1. Why did Paul and Silas sing and pray at midnight (v. 25)? Why is midnight mentioned?

2. What was the content of their prayers?

3. Is there a connection between their prayer and singing and the earthquake that followed immediately (v. 26)?

4. What is the significance of this and all earthquakes? What was the result of this one (v. 26)?

5. After seeing the doors opened and the prisoners freed, what was the jailer's intention (v. 27)? Why would he do this?

6. After Paul stopped him from killing himself, what did the jailer do (vv. 28–30)?

7. What was the jailer's immediate question (v. 30)? How is it to be explained that he asked this question?

8. Does Paul in his answer (v. 31) make faith a condition to salvation? What is the significance of the mention of the jailer's house?

9. What truth is implied in the last part of verse 33? Why was baptism administered immediately?

10. What was the result of this incident (v. 34)?

Acts 16:35–40

These verses record the release of Paul and Silas.

1. Why did the magistrates order the release of Paul and Silas (vv. 35–36)? What did they want the missionaries to do (v. 36)?

2. What was Paul's sharp response (v. 37)? Did the Philippians know that Paul and Silas were Roman citizens (v. 38)? Why were they afraid when Paul told them?

3. What principle is illustrated by Paul's insistence that the magistrates come and release them (v. 37)?

4. Why did Paul insist on being publicly justified?

5. How was the magistrates' attitude now different (v. 39) from what it was earlier (vv. 22–23)?

6. Did Paul and Silas leave Philippi immediately (v. 40)? What did they do before they departed?

Acts 17

Acts 17:1–9

These verses record the events at Thessalonica.

1. What can be said about the city of Thessalonica (v. 1)?

2. Following his custom, where did Paul go (v. 1)? Why? What did he do?

3. What are the scriptures (v. 2)? What was the content of his reasoning with them out of the scriptures (v. 3)?

4. Why did Paul emphasize the necessity of the death and resurrection of Christ (v. 3)?

5. Was the teaching of Paul contrary to the Jews' idea of the Messiah (Christ)?

6. What was the positive fruit among the Jews (v. 4)? What does it mean that some of them consorted with Paul and Barnabas?

7. Did the Greeks (Gentiles) far outnumber the Jews (v. 4)? Why are the chief women especially mentioned? Where were the men?

8. What was the reason that the unbelieving Jews instigated trouble in the city (v. 5)? Of what were they envious?

9. How did the Jews cause an uproar in the city (v. 5)? What is meant by "lewd fellows of the baser sort"? What did they attempt to do (v. 5)?

10. Where were Paul and Barnabas (vv. 5–6)? Who was Jason?

11. What did the Jews do (v. 6)?

12. What accusation did the Jews bring against Paul and Barnabas (vv. 6–7)?

13. How did the rulers of the city solve their problem (v. 9)? What does it mean that they took security of Jason before letting the missionaries go?

Acts 17:10–15

These verses record the history of the church at Berea.

1. Why did the brethren at Thessalonica immediately send Paul and Barnabas to Berea at night (v. 10)? Were they "chickening out" in the face of possible persecution, or was this wisdom? Why?

2. What did Paul immediately do (v. 10)?

3. What does it mean that the Berean Jews were more noble than those of Thessalonica (v. 11)?

4. Of what did this consist (v. 11)? What is meant by readiness of mind?

5. Did the Bereans' searching of scripture imply doubt or suspicion? What are "those things"?

6. What was the connection between searching the scriptures and believing (vv. 11–12)?

7. Why are women again mentioned prominently (v. 12)?

8. Why did the Jews from Thessalonica stir up trouble in Berea (v. 13)?

9. Where did the brethren bring Paul (vv. 14–15)? Why did Paul leave Berea?

10. Why did Silas and Timothy remain in Berea (v. 14) until Paul sent for them (v. 15)?

Acts 17:16–34

These verses record Paul's work in Athens and his sermon on Mars hill.

1. What does it mean that Paul's spirit was stirred in him (v. 16)? Why?

2. Why then did Paul dispute with the Jews and with devout persons (v. 17)? Were they also guilty of idolatry?

3. With whom did Paul dispute in the market (v. 17)? What was this market?

4. Who were the Epicureans (v. 18)?

5. Who were the Stoics (v. 18)?

6. What was the twofold reaction to Paul's teachings (v. 18)? What is the meaning of "babbler"? Why did some call Paul this name?

7. What was the Areopagus (Mars hill) (v. 19)?

8. Why did the Athenians bring Paul there (vv. 19–20)? What did they mean by "new doctrine" and "strange things"? What was their attitude toward the gospel?

9. What was the general characteristic of the Athenians (v. 21)?

10. What did Paul mean in saying that the Athenians were too superstitious (v. 22)?

11. Why did the Greeks build an altar to the unknown God (v. 23)?

12. Were the Athenians ignorantly worshiping God (v. 23)? What is the ignorance of which Paul spoke?

13. Did Paul declare the true God to be what the Athenians worshiped as the unknown god?

14. With what truth did Paul begin to proclaim the knowledge of the true God (vv. 24–26a)?

15. How did Paul reject the idol worship of the Athenians (vv. 24–25)? What could and did they know about the true God (Rom. 1:18ff.)? How did they reject this scriptural teaching?

16. What truth is implied in verses 25b–26?

17. What does it mean that God made of one blood all nations (v. 26)?

18. What was God's purpose in determining the times and places of men (vv. 26–27)?

19. What truth is implied in verses 27–28?

20. To what Greek poet did Paul refer as proof in verse 28? Why did Paul cite him?

21. What conclusion did Paul draw in verse 29? How does he show the impossibility of representing God by images?

22. What did Paul mean by "this ignorance" (v. 30)? Was ignorance an excuse for the heathen's sin? In what sense did God wink at sin?

23. What contrast did Paul draw in verse 30?

24. Why did Paul refer to the final judgment (v. 31)? What connection did he draw between the judgment and the resurrection of Jesus (v. 31)?

25. What was the twofold response of the Athenians (v. 32)?

26. Why did Paul depart from Athens (v. 33)?

27. Who were among the few who believed (v. 34)?

Acts 18

These verses record the establishment of the church at Corinth.

1. Upon leaving Athens and going to Corinth, whom did Paul encounter (vv. 1–2)? Why were they in Corinth?

2. What was the occupation of Aquila and Priscilla (v. 4)? Why did Paul work with them (2 Cor. 11:8–9; 2 Thess. 3:8)? Is this "tent-making" ministry normative for the church?

3. What practice did Paul follow in preaching the gospel (v. 4)?

4. Following the arrival of Timothy and Silas from Macedonia, what did Paul do (v. 5)? What does it mean that Paul was pressed in the Spirit?

5. After the Jews opposed Paul's message and blasphemed (v. 6), what did he do? What does it mean that the Jews' blood would be on their own heads? In what way has this been true in history?

6. To whose house did Paul go (v. 7)? Who was Justus (Acts 1:23)? Why did Paul live with him next to the synagogue?

7. Why is Crispus described as the chief ruler of the synagogue (v. 8)? What was the result of his leadership?

8. Why did God give Paul the vision recorded in verses 9–10?

9. What truth is expressed in verse 10b? What assurance did God give Paul (v. 10b)? Why did he do this?

10. After one and a half years of preaching the gospel without opposition (v. 11), what did the unbelieving Jews do?

11. What charge did the Jews bring against Paul (v. 13)? Who was Gallio? What was his attitude toward the Jews (vv. 14–15)? How did his refusal to render judgment help Paul (vv. 14, 16)?

12. Why did the Greeks beat Sosthenes? How could they get away with doing this (v. 17)?

Acts 18:18–22

These verses record Paul's return to Antioch in Syria via Ephesus.

1. After staying in Corinth for a considerable time, where did Paul go (v. 18)?

2. Can we know what vow Paul made (v. 18)?

3. What did shaving his head have to do with his vow?

4. Did this vow partake of the Old Testament idea of the Nazarite vow?

5. Why did Paul make such a vow?

6. Why did Paul refuse to stay longer in Ephesus (v. 20)?

7. To what feast did Paul refer (v. 21)?

8. Why did Paul want to keep this Old Testament feast, when according to his own preaching the New Testament had come?

9. How did Paul end his second journey (v. 23)?

Acts 18:23–21:17

These verses record Paul's third missionary journey.

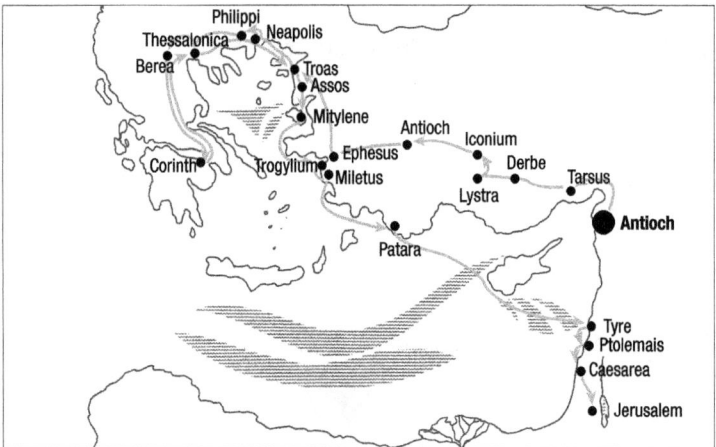

Acts 18:23–19:1

These verses record the start of Paul's third missionary journey.

1. How did Paul begin his third journey (18:23)?

2. What was his immediate goal (19:1)?

Acts 18:24–28

These verses record the person and work of Apollos.

1. What do we know about Apollos (v. 24)?

2. Do we know anything about his earlier instruction (v. 25)?

3. In what way was Apollos' instruction deficient (v. 25)?

4. Was his preaching wrong and heretical, or was it imperfect (v. 26)?

5. How did Aquila and Priscilla help Apollos?

6. What did the brethren at Ephesus do for Apollos (v. 27)? Was this necessary?

7. After going to Achaia, how did he help the church in Corinth (v. 28)?

Acts 19

Acts 19:1–12

These verses record Paul's ministry in Ephesus.

1. Upon arriving in Ephesus (v. 1), what group of twelve men (v. 7) did Paul encounter?

2. In what respect were they deficient (v. 2)? What is meant by receiving the Holy Spirit? Was it not by the work of the Spirit that they had believed?

3. What did these disciples mean in saying that they had not even heard if there was a Holy Spirit?

4. Why did Paul connect the Spirit with baptism (v. 3)?

5. What was the defect in their faith (v. 4)?

6. What did Paul do (v. 6)? What was the result?

7. Why did Paul speak in the synagogue for three months (v. 8)?

8. What is meant by his disputing and persuading? Why did he connect this with the kingdom of God?

9. What is meant by the hardening shown by those of the synagogue (v. 9)? What was the way concerning which they spoke evil? What was Paul's reaction?

10. What was the school of Tyrannus (v. 9)?

11. What was the result of Paul's labor for the next two years (v. 10)?

12. Why did God do special miracles through Paul (v. 11)?

13. Why were handkerchiefs and aprons the means of these miracles (v. 12)?

Acts 19:13–20

These verses record the incident of Sceva.

1. Who were the vagabond Jews (v. 13)? What does it mean that they were exorcists?

2. What did these Jews do (v. 13)? What was their purpose?

3. Why did they use the names of the Lord Jesus and of Paul? Were they successful in casting out the evil spirits (v. 13)?

4. Who was Sceva?

5. Were his sons successful in casting out an evil spirit from a man (v. 15)? What was the negative outcome (v. 16)?

6. What was the purpose of this incident (v. 17)?

7. What were the deeds that many showed (v. 18)?

8. What were the curious arts (v. 19)?

9. Why did the believers burn their books publicly (v. 19)? What was their value?

10. What was the result of these incidents (v. 20)?

Acts 19:21–41

These verses record the riot in Ephesus.

1. Where did Paul now plan to go (v. 21)? What does it mean that he purposed to do this in the Spirit?

2. What route did Paul intend to follow (v. 21)?

3. Whom did he send to Macedonia in the meanwhile (v. 22), while he remained in Asia for a time?

4. What does it mean that there was "no small stir" in Ephesus? What is "that way" (v. 23)?

5. Who was Diana (Greek: Artemis) (v. 24)? How widely was she worshiped (v. 27)? Where was the center of her worship?

6. What was Demetrius' profitable occupation (v. 24)?

7. How was Paul a threat to Demetrius' livelihood? Were Demetrius and his associates concerned primarily with the worship of Diana or with their economic interests (v. 27)?

8. What does this tell us about the growth of the church in this area?

9. How did the riot start (v. 28)? How did it spread (v. 29)? Did anybody know what was happening (v. 29)?

10. Who were Gaius and Aristarchus (v. 29)? Why did the mob seize them and rush to the amphitheater?

11. Why did Paul want to go to the amphitheater (v. 30)? Who prevented him from doing this (v. 31)? Why did they do this?

12. What characterized the mob (v. 32)? How does verse 32 demonstrate the ridiculousness of this riot?

13. How is Alexander described (v. 33)? What did he try to do?

14. What was the response of the mob (v. 34)? What did his being a Jew have to do with putting him to the forefront?

15. Who was the town clerk who finally calmed the screaming mob (v. 35)?

16. What did he assert about the worship of Artemis (Zeus) in relation to the gospel that Paul preached (v. 35)?

17. What advice did he give (vv. 36–37)? How did he defend the Christians (v. 37)?

18. What further utilitarian advice did he give (vv. 40–41)? How did this help the church?

Acts 20

Acts 20:1–6

These verses record the beginning of Paul's return to Jerusalem.

1. After the uproar in Ephesus, where did Paul go (vv. 1–2)?

2. Where did Paul intend to go (v. 3)?

3. Why did he go instead to Macedonia (v. 3)? What churches did Paul visit in Macedonia and Greece? How long was he there (v. 3)?

4. Who were the people who accompanied him (v. 4)?

5. How do we know that Luke joined Paul at Philippi and that together they sailed to Troas (v. 6)?

Acts 20:7–12

These verses record Paul's raising sleepy Eutychus from the dead.

1. What is the significance of the gathering of the believers on the first day of the week (v. 7)?

2. Why did Paul preach until midnight (v. 7)?

3. Where was Eutychus sitting during Paul's sermon (v. 9)? Why did he pick that spot?

4. Did the many lights have anything to do with his falling asleep (v. 8)?

5. Why did Paul fall on him and embrace him (v. 10)?

6. What did Paul mean in saying that his life was in him (v. 10)?

7. What does verse 11 tell us about the church in Troas? What was the topic of their discussion (v. 12)?

Acts 20:13–17

These verses record Paul's journey from Troas to Miletus.

1. How did Paul's companions, including Luke, travel from Troas (v. 13)?

2. Why did Paul travel on foot from Troas?

3. Where did they meet (v. 14)?

4. What route did they take from Assos to Miletus (vv. 14–15)?

5. Why did Paul intend to bypass Ephesus (v. 16)?

6. Why was he in such a hurry?

7. Was the Pentecost mentioned in verse 16 a reference to an Old Testament feast or to the New Testament pouring out of the Holy Spirit?

8. Whom did Paul call to come to him at Miletus (v. 17)? Why did he do this?

Acts 20:18–35

These verses record Paul's farewell speech to the elders of Ephesus.

1. Concerning what did Paul speak in the first part of his address (vv. 18–21)?

2. Why did Paul refer to the manner in which he served the Ephesian church (v. 18)?

3. How did Paul serve the Lord (v. 19)? What is the connection between tears and temptations and the lying in wait of the Jews?

4. How did Paul teach and preach in Ephesus (v. 20)?

5. What was the content of his message (v. 21)? What does this tell us regarding mission work today?

6. Concerning what did Paul speak in the second part of his address (vv. 22–27)?

7. Why did Paul have to go to Jerusalem (v. 22)? What did he expect would happen there (v. 23)? Did he know the details of what would occur there (v. 22)? How did Paul know what would happen there?

8. What was Paul's attitude toward his anticipated problems and persecution (v. 24)?

9. What is the kingdom of God that Paul preached (v. 25)?

10. What message did Paul give the Ephesian elders and church (v. 25)?

11. What admonition did Paul give to the elders (v. 28)?

12. What is the meaning of "take heed" (v. 28)? What is the elders' responsibility?

13. Why is this admonition so serious (vv. 29–30)? From whence will problems arise?

14. What further admonition did Paul give to the church (v. 31)?

15. In the last part of his address how did Paul commend the brethren to God (v. 32)?

16. How does the word of God's grace build up and give an inheritance?

17. Why did Paul use himself as an example regarding material things (vv. 33–34)?

18. What was Paul's final admonition to the church (v. 35)?

Acts 20:36–38

These verses record Paul's final words of farewell.

1. How did the meeting end (vv. 36–37)?

2. What was likely the content of Paul's prayer (v. 36)?

3. Why were the Ephesians most sorrowful (v. 38)?

4. What does this tell us about the relation between Paul and the church at Ephesus?

Acts 21

Acts 21:1–7

These verses record Paul's journey from Miletus to Caesarea.

1. What route did Paul take toward Jerusalem (vv. 1–3)?

2. Which churches did Paul not visit on this return trip? Why not?

3. When Paul spent a week in Tyre, what advice did the church give him (v. 4)? Had he been told this before (Acts 20:23)?

4. Why did the church escort Paul out of the city (v. 6)? What does this tell us about the relation between Paul and the church at Tyre?

5. After leaving Tyre and spending one day in Ptolemais, where did Paul stop next (vv. 7–8)?

Acts 21:8–17

These verses record events in Caesarea.

1. Where did Paul and his companions stay in Caesarea (v. 8)? Who was Philip? Where in Acts was he previously mentioned?

2. What does it mean that Philip's four daughters prophesied (v. 9)? Why is it mentioned that they were virgins? Is there any connection between their being virgins and their prophesying?

3. Is this justification for women officebearers in the church?

4. Who was Agabus (v. 10; Acts 11:28)?

5. What was the symbolism of what Agabus did (v. 11)?

6. What does his prophecy tell us about Paul's intention to go to Jerusalem?

7. What was the reaction of the church (v. 12)? What effect did this have on Paul (v. 13)?

8. How were his companions reconciled to Paul's intention (v. 14)?

9. As they went to Jerusalem, to which early disciple's house did the disciples go (v. 16)?

10. How did the church at Jerusalem receive Paul and his company (v. 17)?

Acts 21:18–26

These verses record the conversation between Paul with his companions and James with the elders of the church at Jerusalem.

1. What was the purpose of this meeting?

2. How did Paul begin the meeting (v. 19)? What does it mean that he declared particularly what God had done among the Gentiles through his ministry (v. 19)?

3. How did the elders introduce their problem (v. 20)?

4. How did they describe the thousands of Jews who had believed? How is it to be explained that these Jews were still zealous in keeping the law?

5. What was Paul's reputation among the Jews (v. 21)? Was this accurate? Where did this conception come from (v. 27)?

6. What urgency did the elders convey to Paul (v. 22)?

7. What was the recommendation of the church at Jerusalem (vv. 23–24)? What was the intent or purpose of this action (v. 24)?

8. Was this a wise course of action? Was this politically motivated? Was this in conflict with the decision of the Jerusalem council (v. 25)?

9. What kind of vow did the four men take (v. 23)? What was necessary when the vow was fulfilled (v. 24)? What was purification? What did the shaving of heads signify?

10. How were the Gentiles separated from this problem (v. 25)?

11. What action did Paul take (v. 26)?

Acts 21:27–40

These verses record a riot in the temple, Paul's arrest by the Romans, and the prelude to his speech in Acts 22.

1. Who were the instigators of trouble for Paul (v. 27)? What did they do?

2. With what did the Jews charge Paul (v. 28)? Was any of this true?

3. What erroneous assumption did they make regarding Trophimus (v. 29)?

4. What did the mob do next regarding the temple (v. 30)?

5. What was the intent of the mob (v. 31)? According to their allegations, why was Paul guilty of death?

6. To whom did news of the riot reach (v. 31)? What was a chief captain? What did he immediately do (v. 32)?

7. What was the result of the interference of the Romans (v. 32)?

8. What did the Roman officer do next (v. 33)? Was this justice, or was it "guilty until proven innocent?"

9. What did the Roman officer do next (v. 34)? Why did he do this?

10. How violent was the mob (vv. 35–36)? How did the officer solve this problem?

11. What did Paul request in his own defense (v. 38)? Why was the Roman officer surprised that Paul spoke Greek?

12. With whom did the Roman confuse Paul (v. 38)?

13. How did Paul correct the captain (v. 39)?

14. What did Paul do next (v. 40)? Why did he speak in the Hebrew (Aramaic) language?

Acts 22–23

Acts 22:1–21

These verses record Paul's speech to the rioting Jews.

1. To what purpose did Paul address his audience as "men, brethren, and fathers" (v. 1)?

2. What point did Paul make by speaking in Hebrew (v. 2)? What was the effect of this?

3. Why did he mention that he was brought up in Jerusalem and at the feet of Gamaliel (v. 3)?

4. How did Paul strengthen his argument that he was a genuine Jew (vv. 4–5)?

5. How did Paul describe his conversion (vv. 6–16)? How did he fill in the details of his conversion as recorded in Acts 9? What point was Paul making in this narrative?

6. Why did Paul mention his vision as part of his defense (v. 17)?

7. What was its content (vv. 18–21)? What did Jesus tell him to do and why (v. 18)? Why did Paul reply as he did (vv. 19–20)?

8. What reason did Jesus give for Paul to leave Jerusalem (v. 21)?

Acts 22:22–29

These verses record Paul's escape from scourging.

1. How did the crowd behave at this time (vv. 22–23)?

2. What was the word that made them so angry that they wanted to kill Paul (v. 21)?

3. Since the Jews proselytized the Gentiles, why were they so upset at Paul's words?

4. What did the chief captain Lysias (23:26) command (v. 24)? What was scourging? What was his purpose? Was this proper justice?

5. What was Roman law on this point (v. 25)? Did this apply only to Roman citizens? How did Paul make his point?

6. Did the Romans have any way of knowing from Paul's speech that he was a citizen?

7. Why did Lysias say that he had bought his citizenship (v. 28)?

8. What immediate action did the Romans take? Why (v. 29)?

Acts 22:30–23:11

These verses record Paul's appearance before the Jewish council.

1. What did Lysias do the next morning (Acts 22:30)? What was the purpose of this meeting? Why was Paul placed before the Sanhedrin?

2. How did Paul begin his defense before the council (v. 1)? What did he mean by having lived in all good conscience before God?

3. Why did this cause Ananias to command that Paul be hit in the mouth (v. 2)?

4. Was this allowed by the law (v. 3)?

5. What was Paul's sharp response (v. 3)? What is the meaning of the "whited wall" that Paul accused Ananias of being?

6. Of what did the Jews accuse him (v. 4)?

7. Was Paul's response in verse 5 sincere or sarcastic?

8. What opportunity did Paul see to divide and conquer (v. 6)? How did Paul define the issue at hand? On which side did he place himself?

9. Did his tactic succeed (v. 7)?

10. What was the difference between the Pharisees and the Sadducees (v. 8)?

11. What was the judgment of the Pharisees (v. 9)? Were they forced into saying more than they wanted to?

12. What did Lysias do at this point (v. 10)? Why?

13. Why did the Lord appear to Paul (v. 11)?

Acts 23:12–24

These verses record the defeat of the Jews' plan to kill Paul and its defeat.

1. What did some of the Jews do the next day (vv. 12–13)? What does it mean that they bound themselves under a curse? How serious was this vow (v. 14)?

2. Who were the co-conspirators (v. 14)?

3. How did they intend to execute their plan (v. 15)?

4. Who was Paul's nephew, and what did he find out (v. 16)? Do we know how he discovered the Jews' plan? Does it matter?

5. What did Paul immediately do (v. 17)?

6. How could Paul get an audience with Lysias without apparent difficulty (vv. 18–19)?

7. What did the young man tell Lysias (vv. 20–21)?

8. With what admonition did Lysias send the young man away (v. 22)?

9. What immediate orders did Lysias give (vv. 23–24)? Why did he order this apparent overkill?

Acts 23:25–30

These verses record the letter from Lysias to Felix.

1. Who was Felix (v. 26)?

2. Why did Lysias write this letter to him?

3. What exaggeration did he use and what falsehood did he tell (v. 27)? Why did he do this?

4. What did Lysias write as to Paul's legal status (v. 29)? Why then did he not release Paul?

5. Of what action did Lysias inform Felix (v. 30)?

Acts 23:31–35

These verses record Paul's journey from Jerusalem to Caesarea.

1. When did this large expedition leave (v. 23)? Why did they travel at night (v. 31)?

2. Why did the infantry return to Jerusalem the next day, while the cavalry escorted Paul the rest of the way (v. 32)?

3. Why did Felix ask what province Paul was from (v. 34)?

4. Where did he keep Paul until his accusers arrived (v. 35)?

Acts 24–25

Acts 24:1–9

These verses record the accusations of the Jews against Paul.

1. Whom did the Jews take with them as their spokesman? Why did not the Jews present their own case?

2. How did Tertullus begin his speech (vv. 2–4)? What was his purpose in doing this?

3. Was there any truth in his words, or was this simply flattery?

4. What charge did Tertullus make in verse 6? Did the Jews have the right to judge Paul according to their law?

5. What were the more serious charges (v. 5)? Whose law did he accuse Paul of violating?

6. Was Tertullus' version of events true (vv. 7–8)?

7. Did Tertullus or the Jews (v. 9) offer any proof for any of his accusations?

Acts 24:10–21

These verses record Paul's defense before Felix.

1. How did Paul's introduction differ from that of Tertullus (v. 10)? Why did Paul mention Felix' long tenure as a judge?

2. Why did Paul emphasize that he had arrived in Jerusalem only twelve days earlier (v. 11)? For what purpose had he come?

3. What charges did Paul deny (v. 12)?

4. Why did Paul flatly deny any possibility of proof for the Jews' charges (v. 13)?

5. Why did Paul describe the God whom he worshiped in the words of verses 14–15?

6. Why did Paul bring up the subject of the resurrection (v. 15)?

7. In contrast to the accusations against him, how did Paul describe himself (v. 16)?

8. What did Paul state as the positive purpose for his presence in Jerusalem (v. 17)?

9. Why did Paul point out the presence of Asian Jews (v. 18)? What charge did he deny?

10. What strong legal point did Paul assert in verse 19?

11. What challenge did Paul issue to his opponents (v. 20)?

12. Why did Paul once again bring up the matter of the resurrection of Jesus (v. 21)?

Acts 24:22–23

These verses record Felix' lack of a decision.

1. What does it mean that Felix had a "more perfect knowledge of that way" (v. 22)?

2. How did he likely have a basic knowledge of the Jews' religion (v. 24)?

3. Why did Felix postpone a decision until he could speak with Lysias? Did he ever consult with Lysias?

4. How was Paul treated during his imprisonment (v. 23)? Why?

Acts 24:24–27

These verses record the further contact between Paul and Felix.

1. Who was Drusilla (v. 24)? Was she Felix' legitimate wife?

2. Why did Felix want to know about the faith in Christ (v. 24)?

3. What is the meaning of righteousness, temperance, and the future judgment (v. 25)?

4. Why did Felix tremble at the words of Paul?

5. Did Felix learn from Paul any righteousness and temperance? What was his course of action?

6. Why did Felix hope for a bribe so that he could release Paul (v. 26)? How did he hope to accomplish this?

7. How long was Paul in custody (v. 27) Why did Felix keep him imprisoned?

Acts 24:27–25:6

These verses record the events leading up to Paul's appearance before Festus.

1. Who was Porcius Festus (24:27)? Where did he establish himself (25:1)?

2. What did the high priest and the Jews do as soon as he assumed office (v. 2)? What did they request (v. 3)? Why did they do this so quickly?

3. What did he instruct the Jews to do (v. 5)?

4. What was the response of Festus (v. 4)? Why did he keep Paul in Caesarea for ten days before holding Paul's trial (v. 6)?

Acts 25:7–12

These verses record Paul's hearing before Festus and his appeal to Caesar.

1. Of what did the Jews accuse Paul (v. 7)?

2. Was the fact that they could not prove their charges a judgment of Luke (the writer of Acts), or was this simply a historical fact?

3. What was Paul's response (v. 8)? Whose two laws did he deny breaking?

4. What did Festus propose as a solution to the problem (v. 9)? What did Festus' willingness to please the Jews indicate about the fairness of the Roman justice system?

5. What did Paul mean by Caesar's judgment seat (v. 10)? Why did he have the right to be judged by the Roman justice system?

6. Was Paul referring to the lower court system or to Caesar himself?

7. What sharp comment did he make to Festus? Is this model appropriate for us?

8.   What did Paul pointedly assert in verse 11?

9.   What was the council that Festus consulted before making his decision (v. 12)?

10. What was Festus' decision (v. 12)?

Acts 25:13–27

These verses record Festus' account to Herod Agrippa of Paul's case.

1.   Who was Agrippa (v. 13)? Where was he king? What was his attitude toward the Jews (v. 19)?

2.   Who was Bernice (v. 13)? How was she related to Agrippa? In light of their relationship, could Agrippa and Bernice render an objective judgment in Paul's case?

3.   Was Festus' account of events accurate? Do verses 15–16 match verses 3–4?

4.   Do verses 19–20 match verse 9?

5. Why did Festus exaggerate his role in these events?

6. What was apparently Festus' main concern (v. 19)?

Acts 25:22–27

These verses record the beginning of Paul's hearing before Agrippa.

1. Why was Agrippa interested in hearing Paul (v. 22)?

2. Who were present at this hearing (v. 23)?

3. Why did Agrippa and Bernice come with great pomp (v. 23)?

4. Was Festus' statement in verse 25 true?

5. What was Festus' problem (vv. 26–27)? How did he hope Agrippa would help him (v. 26)?

Acts 26

Acts 26:1–32

This entire chapter records Paul's address to Agrippa and its result.

Acts 26:1–3

These verses record Paul's introductory remarks.

1. What does it mean that Paul stretched forth his hand (v. 1)?

2. With what words does Paul squarely face the issue at hand (v. 2)?

3. Was Paul flattering Agrippa, or did he sincerely mean his words in verse 3?

4. Did Paul expect to receive justice from Agrippa?

Acts 26:4–8

These verses record Paul's recounting his early life.

1. Why did Paul refer first to his early life (v. 4)?

2. Why did he relate his early life to his present circumstances?

3. Why did Paul mention that he had been a strict Pharisee (v. 5)?

4. How did Paul define the issue (vv. 6–7)?

5. What was the "hope of the promise" (v. 6)?

6. Why did Paul speak of the resurrection of the dead in this connection (v. 8)?

Acts 26:9–12

These verses record the history of Paul's persecution of the Christians.

1. How did Paul recount his persecution of the Christians?

2. What does it mean that he compelled them to blaspheme (v. 11)?

3. What does it mean that Paul was exceedingly mad against the Christians (v. 11)?

4. To what extreme did he go (v. 12)?

5. Why did Paul go into such detail regarding his previous life?

Acts 26:13-18

These verses record Paul's account of his conversion.

1. How does Paul's account (vv. 13–15) differ from other accounts?

2. What aspect of his conversion did Paul emphasize (vv. 16–18)? Why did he do this?

3. What were the things in which Jesus would appear to Paul (v. 16)?

4. What is the inheritance among those who are sanctified (v. 18)? Who are the sanctified?

Acts 26:19–21

These verses record Paul's obedience to the commission he had received.

1. What did Paul assert (v. 19)?

2. Why did Paul make a point of the order in which he preached the gospel (v. 20)?

3. What are "works meet for repentance" (v. 20)?

4. What were the causes for which the Jews tried to kill Paul (v. 21)?

Acts 26:22–23

These verses record Paul's summary of the gospel that he preached.

1. What is Paul's main point in summarizing his preaching and teaching (v. 22)?

2. What was his purpose in citing Moses and the prophets (v. 22)?

3. What did Paul assert to be the content of Moses and the prophets (v. 23)?

4. Who are the people to whom Paul refers in verse 23?

Acts 26:24–29

These verses record the concluding conversation among Paul, Festus, and Agrippa.

1. Why did Felix loudly interrupt Paul (v. 24)? What did he say about Paul's mental state? What did he assert was the cause of this?

2. How did Paul respectfully contradict Festus (v. 25)?

3. What are the words of truth and soberness?

4. How did Paul characterize Agrippa's knowledge of these past events (v. 26)? What reason did he give?

5. In addressing Agrippa directly, what question did Paul ask and answer (v. 27)? Did Agrippa really believe the prophets? If Paul's assertion is correct, in what sense was this true?

6. Was Agrippa's response in verse 28 sincere, or was it sarcastic?

7. In this connection does the hymn "Almost Persuaded" correctly represent Agrippa's words?

8. For what did Paul wish in his response (v. 29)? Is almost good enough?

Acts 26:30–32

These verses record the private judgment among Festus, Agrippa, and Bernice.

1. Why did they reach their verdict privately?

2. What was their (correct) conclusion (v. 31)?

3. What was Agrippa's conclusion (v. 32)? Could Paul's appeal have been undone?

4. Did Festus now have something to write to Caesar regarding the reason for sending Paul to Rome?

Acts 27

Acts 27:1–44

This entire chapter records most of Paul's journey to Rome.

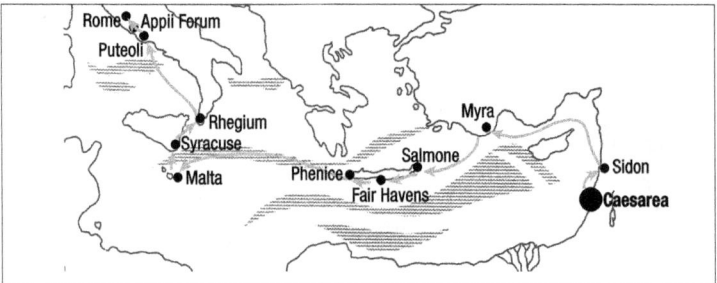

1. Why did the Holy Spirit through Luke recount the details of Paul's lengthy journey to Rome?

2. How is this gospel? Do the details of Paul's journey really matter?

Acts 27:1–8

These verses record Paul's journey from Jerusalem/Caesarea to the Fair Havens.

1. How do we know that Luke was travelling with Paul at this time (v. 1)?

2. In whose custody did Paul travel (v. 1)?

3. Who was Aristarchus (v. 2)? Where was he going?

4. What opportunity was Paul given at Sidon (v. 3)? Why did Julius give Paul liberty? Who were his friends?

5. What does it mean that they sailed under Cyprus (v. 4)? Why did they do this?

6. Why did they sail along the coast of Asia (v. 5)?

7. What route did they take toward the Fair Havens (v. 8)?

Acts 27:9–44

These verses record the storm Paul and the ship encountered after leaving the Fair Havens.

1. Why was it dangerous to sail after much time had passed (v. 9)?

2. How could Paul know that sailing at this time was dangerous to the ship, its cargo, and the lives of its occupants (v. 10)? What was the ship's cargo (v. 38)?

3. Whose opinion prevailed (v. 11)?

4. Why did they sail from the Fair Havens (v. 12)?

5. What attempt did they make (v. 12)?

6. What encouraged them to try to sail to Crete (v. 13)?

7. What happened next (v. 14)? What was Euroclydon?

8. In what direction did they need to go? Why could they not head in that direction (v. 15)? What did they do? What does it mean that they let her drive?

9. What was their problem (v. 16)?

10. What does it mean that they used helps and undergirded the ship (v. 17)? Why did they do this? What happened when they took down (strake) the sails?

11. What did they do when the storm did not abate (v. 18)?

12. What further action did they take (v. 19)?

13. How severe was this storm (v. 20)?

14. What is the long abstinence of verse 21? Was Paul engaging in "I told you so"?

15. What promise did Paul make to his shipmates (v. 22)?

16. How could he do this (v. 23)?

17. What reason did he give (v. 24)? How was this a reason that all would be saved (v. 24)?

18. What assurance did Paul give (v. 25)?

19. However, what would be the way that they would be saved (v. 26)?

20. How long and how far were they driven by the storm (v. 27)?

21. What did the sailors sense during the night (v. 27)?

22. What did they do to confirm their thinking (v. 28)? How deep was the water as they approached land (v. 28)?

23. What did the sailors do in order to hold their position (v. 29)?

24. What was the intention of the sailors (v. 30)? Under what ruse did they intend to escape in the ship's lifeboat?

25. What did Paul tell Julius the centurion was necessary that everyone needed to stay in the ship (v. 33)? What did the soldiers do (v. 32)?

26. To what abstinence did Paul refer (v. 33)? What was the reason or fasting for fourteen days? Why did Paul give this advice (v. 34)?

27. What example did Paul set (v. 35)? How did they follow his example?

28. Why is it noted at this point that the ship contained 276 souls (v. 37)?

29. After lightening the ship (v. 38), what was the intention of the sailors (v. 39)?

30. Why did this plan not work (vv. 40–41)?

31. What was the intention of the soldiers (v. 42)? Why would they do this?

32. Why did the centurion stop them (v. 43)? How did the prisoners get to shore (vv. 43–44)?

Acts 28

Acts 28:1-6

These verses record Paul's survival of a viper attack.

1. Where had the ship finally landed (v. 1)?

2. What does it mean that the inhabitants were a barbarous people (v. 2)?

3. How did they treat the ship's occupants (v. 2)?

4. How did the natives interpret the viper bite (v. 4)?

5. After nothing happened to Paul, how did they change their minds (v. 6)?

6. What is the reason for this narrative? Was there any saving effect?

Acts 28:7–10

These verses record many miracles of healing.

1. Who was Publius (v. 7)? How did he treat the shipwrecked visitors?

2. What was wrong with his father?

3. How did Paul heal him (v. 8)?

4. What was the effect of this healing (v. 9)? Was the gospel also preached?

5. How did the Maltese show their gratitude (v. 10)?

Acts 28:11–16

These verses record Paul's journey from Malta to Rome.

1. Why did they stay in Malta for three months (v. 11)?

2. On what ship did they travel to Rome (v. 11)? What is the significance of the sign of Castor and Pollux? What route did they take?

3. How could Paul as a prisoner stay for seven days in Puteoli (v. 14)?

4. Who came to meet him in Apii forum and the Three Taverns (v. 15)? Why did Paul need courage?

5. What special privilege did Paul receive in Rome (v. 16)? How is this to be explained?

Acts 28:17–29

These verses record Paul's dealings with the Jews in Rome.

1. Whom did Paul call together (v. 17)?

2. How did he explain his presence in Rome (vv. 17–19)?

3. What reason did Paul give for speaking with the Jews (v. 20)?

4. Did the Jews know anything at all about Paul (v. 21)? Why not?

5. What did the Jews say about the Christian religion (v. 22)? Why did they call it a sect? What is a sect?

6. Concerning what and whom did Paul preach the gospel (v. 23)? How did he support his exposition and testament?

7. What was the two-fold result of his preaching (v. 24)?

8. What prophecy did Paul apply to the unbelieving Jews (vv. 25–27)? To what did he ascribe their unbelief?

9. With what message did Paul conclude (v. 28)? What was the reaction of the Jews (v. 29)?

Acts 28:30–31

These verses conclude the book of Acts.

1. Where did Paul live in Rome (v. 30)? Why was he not in prison instead of under house arrest?

2. What did Paul do for at least two years (v. 31)? What was the heart of his message?

3. How was it possible for Paul to preach boldly and freely?

Concluding Questions

The introduction to this study guide stated a three-fold theme found in Acts: it is the history of the work of the Holy Spirit; it sets forth the doctrine of the church; and it records the spread of the gospel through the preaching. Having completed the study of Acts, how would you summarize each of these three themes?

1. Trace the work of the Holy Spirit in the history of the church.

2. How does Acts teach the doctrine of the church?

3. Show the history of the preaching and the spread of the gospel.

Notes